GW00739051

BRIGHT · SPARK

We can shape it

Rosie Dalzell

Photographs: Zul Mukhida

Series Consultant: Sue Dale Tunnicliffe

Geddes+ Grosset

First published in hardback 1991
Copyright © Cherrytree Press Ltd 1991 and
Touchstone Publishing Ltd 1991

This paperback edition first published 1991 by
Geddes & Grosset Ltd
David Dale House
New Lanark, ML11 9DJ

ISBN 1 85534 451 3

Printed and bound by
Proost N.V., Turnhout, Belgium

Contents

Projects

Words

Difficult words are explained on p. 26.

Check

Before you start any project, check to see if there is a safety note (marked !) in the text. This means you need an adult to help you.

Paper polygons

Sam is making mobiles from paper shapes. Which shapes is he using? Start by drawing a line from the outside of your shape towards the centre, then cut along it.

Make a mobile like Sam's. When you've cut along your line, you can hang it up. Where does the thread go?

Try cutting folded paper too. Sam cut the snowflakes on the lampshade and the dancers out of folded paper.

! **You'll need sharp scissors – mind your fingers.**

◀**This monster has been folded and cut so that it pops up when Sam opens the book.**

Dress designer

What outfits can you design for a football team or a wedding party? Fit them on card dolls to see how they look.

Rachel and Alvin are trying out all kinds of fabrics — fluffy, shiny, thick, stretchy, patterned and plain.

Which shapes and fabrics will you choose for your designs?

! **Get an adult to help you cut out the card dolls.**

▶**This tailor is cutting out pieces of cloth to make a man's suit. He will fit it on the dummy to see how it looks.**

6

Creative casting

Make a **plaster** cast of a sand picture or the letters of your name. Sam is pouring plaster mixed with water on to Jenna's mould. What is the card shape for?

When the plaster has set, they can lift up their cast, brush the sand off gently as it dries, and paint it.

Everything will come out back to front, so write your name backwards, in mirror writing. Which letter has Jenna written the wrong way round in her sand mould?

! **Wrap up plaster leftovers and put them in the bin.**

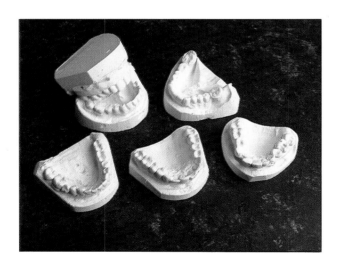

◀Dentists use plaster casts to make false teeth. The patient bites into a modelling material to make the mould.

Plastic possibilities

What kind of model can you make using empty plastic bottles, bags, packaging, pots and straws and . . . what else?

Gemma's dessert pot is easy to shape with scissors. What is Dean using to cut the polystyrene tile?

Try some glues and tapes to see which ones will stick plastic. Gemma used plasticine to hold up her masts and flags. What models can you make for your toys?

! **Get an adult to help you cut things.**

▶ **Plastics can be moulded into lots of different shapes. Look round your home to see what you can find.**

Clay cut-outs

Stacey has made these colourful patterns from small clay tiles fitted closely together. Can you see which shape she has used for each pattern?

Choose a shape and cut tiles out of a sheet of clay, as Stacey has done. If you roll the clay out on paper, the tiles can dry on it and keep their shape.

Now you can paint them and invent your own patterns.

! **Clay is messy – it's best to wear an overall.**

◀**Thousands of tiny clay tiles were needed to make this** mosaic **floor, laid by the Romans 1,600 years ago.**

Mushy mâché

Gemma and Dean have made puppet heads and some tiny furniture out of **papier mâché**. They tore up newspaper, poured on lots of hot water and left the mixture to soak.

Then they poured away the water and mashed the paper pulp with flour and water glue. What is Dean making now? What could you make with some papier mâché?

Papier mâché models take a few days to dry. Then you can paint or **varnish** them.

► **Papier mâché makes light, strong objects which are easy to decorate. It also makes good egg boxes.**

Monster jelly

Have you made jelly before? Ask an adult to boil some water and stir in the jelly cubes. How do you know when the jelly is ready to pour into a mould?

Ice cube trays, yogurt pots, old plastic packaging, egg cups, shells and lots of other things all make unusual moulds. What can you find to shape your jelly?

Stacey has made a monster. When your jellies have set turn them out to make an exciting picture.

◄Gelatine **was poured on to this food and allowed to set. It can now be sliced like a cake.**

Metal models

Rachel and Alvin have made all these **sculptures** with different metals. What metals can you find to work with?

Can you tear your metals or cut them with scissors? Alvin is using wire cutters for some thicker wire.

Which metals will bend to make a firm shape? Rachel wound wire round a broom handle to make a bubble blower. Now she is coiling a curly spring round a pencil.

! **Be careful of sharp edges. Put a cork on the wire end.**

►**This machine cuts and shapes sheets of printed metal to make milk bottle tops.**

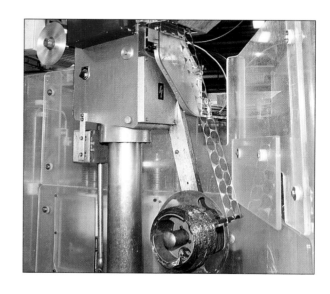

Seal a secret

Candle wax melts easily and goes solid quickly as it cools. Can you press a pattern in it, just as it sets?

Rosie is putting a spoonful of melted wax on the back of Stacey's envelope to seal it. Stacey will press a plastic letter in the wax to make a pattern.

Design your own wax seal for your letters and parcels. Melt a crayon with the wax to colour it.

! **You need an adult to help you with the hot wax.**

◀**Candles are made by dipping** wicks **many times into molten wax. Some have patterns pressed into the warm wax.**

21

Fancy dress

Rachel and Alvin are making dressing-up clothes. Is there enough material to make a witch's skirt for Rachel?

They are using elastic thread to sew the fabrics. The elastic stretches, so the clothes will be easy to get on and off.

Alvin is sewing along the edge of some red net. He will pull the thread to make a ruff, like the one on the floor. What could you make with elastic thread?

! **Make sure the needle doesn't go through your finger.**

▶ **All dressed up for the party. Watch out witch – here comes a custard pie!**

It's a frame-up

Sam and Jenna are making picture frames. How many pieces of wood do they need for each picture? How can they make sure the frame is the right shape for the picture?

Jenna is sawing the wood, using a **vice** to keep the wood steady. What is Sam doing?

Wood glue will stick the sides of the frame together. When it is dry, Jenna and Sam can glue the painting on to the back and hang it up with string and drawing pins.

! **Get an adult to help you cut things.**

◀ **Pictures in an art gallery have all kinds of different frames.**

Words to remember

Gelatine   A pale yellow solid made by boiling animal bones and skin. Jelly is made with powdered gelatine.

Mosaic   A picture or design made with small pieces of clay, stone or glass of different colours.

Papier mâché   Paper made into a pulp, mixed with glue and used for making models, boxes, bowls etc.

Plaster   A white powder (containing calcium sulphate) that sets after it has been mixed with water.

Sculpture   The art of shaping objects or statues from stone, wood, metal or any other material.

Varnish   A clear liquid which is painted on a surface and dries to give a hard, shiny finish.

Vice   Tool, usually made of iron, attached to a bench which can grip things and hold them steady.

Wick   The strip of material which you light in a candle or a paraffin or oil lamp.

Books for you

Wood, by Terry Jennings (Threads Series, A & C Black)
Plastics, by Terry Jennings (A & C Black)
Clay, by Annabelle Dixon (A & C Black)

Books to look at with an adult

The Art and Craft of Papier Mâché by Juliet Bawden (Mitchell Beazley)
Clothes and Costume, by Doug Kincaid and Peter Coles (Hulton)

Places to go

Summerlee Heritage Trust, West Canal Street, Coatbridge, Strathclyde ML5 1QD. Ironworks, workshops, etc.
Ironbridge Gorge Museum, Ironbridge, Telford TF8 7AW, Shropshire. A cluster of industrial museums including *Blists Hill Open Air Museum* and *Coalport China Works Museum*.
Victoria and Albert Museum, South Kensington, London SW7 2RL. Costume displays, papier mâché, pottery, etc.
Porthmadog Pottery, Snowdon Street, Porthmadog, Gwynedd. Watch potters at work and make and paint your own pot.
Ulster Folk Museum, Cultra Manor, Holywood, Co Down, BT18 0EU. An old forge and a water-powered spade mill.

Sparky ideas

Here are some background facts for adults along with some talking points and more ideas to try together.

pp 4–5 Paper polygons
- Experiment with different kinds of paper. Talk about which ones are strong, and which are easy to cut, draw on, see through. How do these properties affect their uses?
- Point out other things made from paper shaped by cutting, eg paper doilies and cards.

pp 6–7 Dress designer
- Talk about each fabric: is it made from synthetic or natural fibres, or a mixture? Natural fibres either come from animals (wool and silk) or plants (cotton and linen). Most synthetic fibres are plastics made from petroleum oil.
- Is the fabric woven, knitted, or pressed together (like felt)? Has it been dyed or printed?

pp 8–9 Creative casting
- Make the plaster of Paris by adding the powder to water (usually about 1½ times more powder than water by volume). Moulding plaster or plaster filler work too. Use *damp* sand for the mould.
- When water is added, the plaster (calcium sulphate) forms crystals which bind together as it sets.
- Cornices and ceiling roses may be made of plaster.
- Plaster is also mixed with sand to smooth brick walls and hardens bandages to bind up broken limbs.

pp 10–11 Plastic possibilities
- 'Plastic' just means easily shaped. Modern plastics can be engineered with virtually any set of properties and

increasingly take the place of traditional materials.

• Unfortunately, plastics are much more difficult to dispose of and recycle than the materials they have replaced. The fossil fuels they are made from will soon run out. We may have to rethink our dependence on them.

pp 12–13 Clay cut-outs

• Stacey's patterns, made of identical shapes which fit together exactly, are called tessellations. Look at them in tiled areas on floors and walls. You may also find tessellations which use more than one regular shape.

• Try making a mosaic pattern (like the Roman one in the photograph), or a picture, from *irregular* clay shapes.

pp 14–15 Mushy mâché

• Papier mâché shrinks as it dries, so finger holes in puppet heads have to be roomy.

• Explain that the newspaper was originally made from wood and the papier mâché process turns it back into something hard and strong.

• Paper has been recycled like this for centuries to make anything from toys and dolls to furniture and masks.

• Often strips of paper are pasted individually into a mould. You can try this, using a balloon or plate base.

pp 16–17 Monster jelly

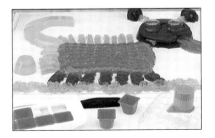

• Gelatine is made by boiling animal tissue and bones.

• For jelly modelling, use a little less water than usual.

• Make your own healthy, additive-free jellies by adding gelatine, dissolved in warm water, to fresh fruit juices.

pp 18–19 Metal models

• The metals here are iron (wire, wool, food can), aluminium (foil, drink can) and copper wire. The paper clips and fasteners are iron coated with brass.

- Iron is everywhere, but because it rusts easily, it is often painted, coated with other metals or treated to make stainless steel. Aluminium is light so it is used in aeroplanes, and as a wrapping material. Water pipes and electricity wires are made of copper.
- Test metals with a magnet to see which contain iron.

pp 20–21 Seal a secret
- Heat the wax *carefully* in a bowl over a saucepan of simmering water or, preferably, in a double boiler until it has just melted. Talk about the differences between the liquid wax (flows, takes the shape of its container, transparent) and the solid (fixed shape, opaque).
- Explain that in the past people would seal their post with wax, not glue.

pp 22–23 Fancy dress
- Thin elastic thread, a needle with a big eye and loosely woven fabrics are best for this activity.
- Look in the library and museums for ideas to adapt for other simple costumes.

pp 24–25 It's a frame-up
- Instead of a vice, you could use a bench hook or mitre board (there is one in the picture). You will need a strong wood adhesive. Try smoothing the frame with sandpaper before you glue it together. Find out which grade (coarseness) of paper works best.
- The wood (1 cm square softwood available from timber merchants in various lengths) will have come from under the bark of a fast-growing conifer tree. Feel the smooth grain running the length of the wood (parallel to the tree's trunk) and the rough cross-grain at the sawn ends. Look for knots where a branch joined the trunk.
- **Extra safety note:** Be aware of the glue-sniffing problem.

Index

Thank you!

The author would like to thank junior technologists Andrew, Charlie, Ellen Rose, Emily, Francesca, Kate, Laura and Samuel for their work on the projects; and Sam, Rachel, Alvin, Jenna, Dean, Gemma and Stacey for appearing in the photographs. Thanks are also due to the teaching staff of St John the Baptist RC First School, Davigdor Infants School, St Bartholomew's CE First School and St Luke's Terrace First School, all of Brighton, for their patience and co-operation, and to Hove Museum and Art Gallery for allowing us to photograph picture frames. The woodwork tools were lent to us by Technical Teaching Services.

The author would also like to thank Hugh and her own children, Thomas, Kate and Harry, for all their help and encouragement.

Picture credits

The projects were all photographed specially by Zul Mukhida. Other pictures were supplied by: Topham Picture Source pp. 6, 16; ZEFA p. 20 (V. Wentzel); Zul Colour Library, pp. 8, 12, 18, 24.